Taming the
Technology Monster

Taming the Technology Monster

8 GUIDING PRINCIPLES FOR RAISING DIGITAL NATIVES

Sissy Goff, LPC-MHSP

ISBN: 1543091946
ISBN 13: 9781543091946

Taming the Technology Monster

§

A TEENAGER IN COUNSELING RECENTLY told me, "My phone is like my heart monitor. If I don't have it, I'll die."

A parent in counseling recently told me, "What lice is to parents of elementary schoolers, technology is to parents of middle schoolers."

Both often, and sadly, can be true. When I started teaching a class for parents on technology, I decided to name it *Taming the Technology Monster*. It feels like that. But I also know that there are some who would say I'm vilifying technology with that title. So, I often refer to it as Taming our Little Monsters while they Use Technology, because that's what it sometimes degenerates into…especially when you're trying to talk your ten year-old son into turning off his video console.

From the outset, I have to say that I'm writing this as a counselor, not an IT person. I understand enough myself to operate my own phone, tablet, and yes, I do have a smart watch. But that's about as techie as I get. I don't understand the world of technology. But, after counseling children and adolescents for almost 25 years, I do mostly understand the world of kids. And parents. And how technology has completely changed the landscape.

As a result, I have come up with 8 Guiding Principles for Raising Digital Natives—in other words, 8 of what I consider, as a counselor, the most important ideas we need to know to understand and help the kids we love when it comes to technology.

CHAPTER 1

Technology is here to stay.

§

TODAY'S GENERATION OF KIDS HAVE several names: digital natives, the iGeneration, the selfie generation, and a host of others names revolving around technology. They are the first generation of kids who will have technology as a *prominent* force in their daily lives as long as they can remember. And it is a prominent force. For example, the average person checks their screens every 9 minutes and 50 seconds during their waking hours each day.[1] Adults spend an average of 10 hours and 39 minutes per day consuming media on screens.[2] If those are the statistics for adults, what about these digital natives? According to one source, kids under the age of two average 53 minutes per day on screens. For two to four year olds, it rises to 2 ½ hours per day. Five to eight year olds spend approximately 3 hours per day on their screens.[3] The American Academy of Pediatrics says that children, across the board, spend an average of 7 hours per day on entertainment related media.[4] Teenagers are averaging 9 hours per day on their screens.[5] And get this: 69% of children between the ages of 2-5 can use a computer mouse, but only 11% can tie their own shoes. 58% of children know how to play a video game, while 52% know how to ride a bike, and only 20% know how to swim.[6]

Something's off. It's off in terms of how today's generation of kids are spending their time, and it's off in terms of how its impacting their brains.

CHAPTER 2

Technology is literally re-wiring the brains of the kids we love.

ALL OF OUR BRAINS GROW in response to how they're being used—as we get older, they just grow less (and work less, too, according to myself and anyone else over the age of 40). Between birth and two years of age, an infant's brain triples in size. It continues in a state of rapid development until the age of 21. Early brain development is largely determined by environmental stimuli.

As we know, an overexposure to technology is associated with childhood obesity and diabetes, from a physical standpoint. In terms of a child's brain development, it's associated with diagnoses of ADHD, autism, coordination disorder, developmental delays, learning difficulties, and sensory processing disorder. From an emotional standpoint, it's also seen as a causal factor in anxiety and depression in children, as well as increased impulsivity and a decreased ability to self-regulate.[7]

As all of us who love teenagers know that their brains are in constant flux, as well. Although by the age of six, the brain is already 95% of the size of an adult brain, the gray matter continues to grow throughout adolescence. The brain cells are growing extra connections, causing a period of rapid growth and thickening of the gray matter, which is considered the thinking part of the brain. This process peaks at approximately age

11 for girls and age 12 for boys. From then on, the excess connections are what scientists refer to as "pruned." It's literally like the gardening term, meaning that what is being used survives and flourishes, whereas the cells and connections not used wither and die. They call it the "use it or lose it" principle.[8] This doesn't bode well for the teens who are spending 9 hours per day on screens for entertainment purposes (as opposed to screens for educational purposes).

Socially, we all know the implications of this hyper-focus on technology. The overexposure creates a lack of time for relationships and delays their social skills learning. They, and we, basically learn social skills by being social. In a study conducted at UCLA, 6th graders who went 5 days without screens were significantly better at reading human emotions than those who were continuing their regular use with their devices.[9]

In addition, an overexposure to technology impacts a child's creativity—and ours probably, too. Think about it: where and when do you have your most creative thoughts? When we ask parents at our technology classes, their answers are typically "in the shower," "waking up," and "falling asleep"—times we typically aren't looking at a screen. It is in those times that we have what we call "aha moments." In other words, we have more creative thoughts when our minds aren't engaged elsewhere.

So, what can we do?

Research says there are four critical factors necessary for our children to develop: movement, touch, human connection, and exposure to nature. All four factors foster coordination, self-regulation, and many other skills necessary for school entry. Young children's brains need 2-3 hours per day of active play to achieve adequate sensory stimulation.[10] As children grow older, those same four factors are crucial. Teenagers need to move, to connect with others in real time, and to be hugged (no matter how much they stiff-arm us with their embarrassed selves). They need time outdoors—to help them stretch their legs, minds, and the self-preoccupation that accompanies life on social media.

Technology not only impacts, but changes the way the kids we love grow and develop. Screens can be helpful in furthering their growth in certain areas, too—an idea we'll come back to later. But we want children to put down their screens so that their exposure is limited to technology, but heightened to real life—where connection, creativity, relationships and the things that matter most really occur.

CHAPTER 3

You are the gatekeeper.

§

NONE OF US WOULD ALLOW our eight year-old to walk into an adult bookstore. But, in effect, that's precisely what we're doing when we allow them to use technology without any type of monitoring. Statistically, 60% of parents do not supervise their child's technology usage.[11] Although those numbers concern me greatly, I do understand.

I recently met with a mom who had lost her husband. She had three children, and an elementary aged daughter who had just looked at pornography for the first time. "I know I'm supposed to have all of this stuff on the computer so I know what they're doing. I honestly just haven't had the energy, and I thought she was young enough that we were safe."

No matter what your situation is as a parent, you are probably exhausted. All parents are, in different (maybe most) seasons. But, your child is not. He or she is curious and quick and likely already more adept at using technology than you are. And, think about it... What do you do when you wonder something? You google it. If you were a child, wouldn't you prefer googling what a body part is supposed to look like to having an awkward conversation with your parent?

At Daystar, we have children as young as eight who are addicted to pornography. You are the gatekeeper for your child. You have to be willing to be the bad guy. Your child—yes, even your teenager needs parents more than they need followers. Here are a few gatekeeping ideas:

* *If your child gets the privilege, you get to set the boundaries.* Years ago, I taught my first parenting class on technology. It was when Facebook was first becoming a thing. (Now, they leave Facebook to us "old people" and have moved on to Snapchat and Instagram. By the time you read this, they'll have likely moved on to something else.) I told these parents that they needed to be watching closely from the first moments that their children started using social media. In fact, they needed to more than "friend" their kids in the beginning: they needed to have their passwords (an idea I still advocate, no matter what social media platform your children are using.). As their friend, you can't check their incoming and outgoing private messages, which is sometimes where the trouble occurs. A mom spoke up from the corner of the room and said, "There's no way my son will give me his password. He won't even accept my friend request." Now, her problem was clearly bigger than just technology use in her home. It was a respect and authority issue at the deepest level. Kids can and will try to argue this point, especially if they paid or helped pay for their phone or gadget. Don't be dissuaded. You are still the gatekeeper, *even* if they've paid for all or a portion of their device. If it's under your roof, you ultimately are in control.

* *You have to be ahead of the game.* Before you allow your child to download an app, download it yourself first. Play it and determine if it has a social media component. Many games and apps do, but parents don't notice until too late—because the interactive portion is placed at the very bottom of the page. And don't necessarily rely on the age recommendations given by the online store.

* *Supervise video chatting.* If your child is talking to someone else via Skype or Facetime or some other video platform, have them

chat in a central location in your home. Because chatting is not recorded, it can be a place where kids feel freer to say or do things they wouldn't if they knew their parents were watching. You can monitor less as they get older, but young ones should always be supervised, unless they're chatting with a grandparent or other trusted adult.

* *Link your email to their iTunes or Google account.* You want to be aware of what apps they're downloading. If their account is set up under your email address, you will be able to check on what they've installed on their devices. Many smartphones and tablets also have a setting that disables the user's ability to delete apps. You want to turn this setting on, so your child can't download an app and then delete it right before they hand their phone to you. (Can you tell I've heard that story a time or two in my office?)

* *Put filters and monitoring systems on your computers and gadgets,* including yours if you allow them to use it. Filters prevent inappropriate content from reaching them. Monitoring systems keep you informed as to what they are doing and communicating online and via text.

Some of our favorite resources include:

* Teen Safe, teensafe.com
* Zabra, zabra.com
* mSpy, mSpy.com
* Mama Bear, mambearapp.com
* Curbi, curbi.com
* Family Protector, intego.com
* KidsWatch, kidswatch.com
* Disney Circle, meetcircle.com
* Safe Eyes, internetsafety.org
* Covenant Eyes, covenanteyes.com
* Common Sense Media, commonsensemedia.org

- Technology Tuesday's at raisingboysandgirls.com (which happens to be our blog)

Also, check out the American Academy of Pediatrics site to create a specialized media plan for your family at healthy children.org.

Thankfully, these sites and other great ones offer help in keeping our kids protected. You want to do your own research to make sure the software you choose is right for your family and the devices and social media they use.

CHAPTER 4
Start small.

§

Every time we speak to parents about technology, someone asks the question: "When should I let my child have _____?" In other words, what's the magic age? When will he be old enough to be responsible? When will she be mature enough to make good choices? Unfortunately, there is no magic age. But, there are some guidelines that we, and the good folks at the American Academy of Pediatrics would strongly suggest.

- *When?* Our answer to that question is to parent in community. Basically, you want a group of like-minded parents walking this road with you. You can decide together when you're going to let your kids have their first email account, or their first cell phone, or Instagram account, or whatever the shiny new penny of the day is. That way, when your child says, "All the other kids have _____, (which your child will say at some point), you can say, "That's funny, because I know the Smith's and the Johnson's or (whomever your home team is) don't have those yet either." Basically, you have automatic back up.

  In addition, you don't want your child to be the first and you don't want them to be the last. If they're the first, they'll often be perceived as the frontrunner—or fast—as we would say when I was growing up. Others will see them as on the cutting edge. Basically, you don't want your child to be on the cutting edge of growing up. It's too risky and the cutting edge gets scarier as they get older. But, if they're the last to have all things technology, they'll often be the ones who rebel. They'll sneak, "borrow" a friend's device. Or, they'll be left behind. The reality is that, for teenagers, social media has become how they communicate. Now, we believe you can let your child be second or even next to last, rather than the very last. We also have parents at Daystar who choose one item to delay. We have plenty of parents who don't let their kids have smartphones till 16, with the message that a phone is a convenience for the parent, not the child. Or, we have parents who hold off on Snapchat, or some other hot ticket item. But, if you hold off on all things technology, your child will often find their way to it without your knowledge—and rebel. Plus, the goal of taming the technology monster is to teach them responsible technology use while they're under our roofs.

* *How much?* In 2016, the American Academy of Pediatrics changed their guidelines. Up to that point, it was no screen time at all for kids under the age of 2. Now, it's no screen time for children under the age of 18 months. It used to also be no more than 2 hours per day of screen time for kids under the age of 18. Now, they say 1 hour for kids under the age of 6, and they don't give any guidelines past that age, other than "place consistent limits on the time spent using media, and the types of media, and make sure media does not take the place of adequate sleep, physical activity and other behaviors essential to health."[12] Basically, they're saying it's up to the parent's guidance and discretion. However, the brain development of children did not magically change in the year 2016. They adjusted their numbers knowing the prevalence and sometimes helpfulness of technology today. We still need to be good guides.

* *Require 10 minutes of rest for every 90 minutes of tech.* Researchers say children need 10 minutes of rest for every 90 minutes of technology use.[12] It helps their brain development and calms the overactivity of the brain that can develop using screens.

- *Stop using technology 30 to 60 minutes before bed.* We've all read the data on technology related sleep disturbances. I taught a technology class where one teenager said she had to have her ipad by her bed, because it was how she read her Bible. I tried to explain to her that there had been beautiful, leather-bound, hardback, and even paperback versions of the Bible that had been around for quite some time, and work just as well.
- *Have screen free zones in your home, including mealtime.* We have cell phone baskets in our counseling offices at Daystar. You can have them in your dining room, or at the kitchen table. But, have some space where everyone collectively unplugs for the purpose of connection.
- *Keep computers in common spaces.* For as long as possible, keep the computer your child uses in a room you frequent. It's good accountability for them to know that you regularly enter the space where they're using technology.
- *Have a central plug in station in your bedroom.* Kids really don't need their gadgets in their room after bedtime. I've heard story after story of teenagers who send inappropriate texts and pictures after everyone in the house has gone to bed. They need to plug them in somewhere centrally located, preferably in a room where you'll notice if they sneak them out. (Can you tell I've heard that one before, too? Hallways and kitchens are all too accessible.)
- *Take technology sabbaths together.* We know plenty of families who have screen-free Sundays, or weekends, or even spring breaks together. If the idea of a technology sabbath causes you to perspire just a bit, it might be time to think about your own technology use.
- *Give them more freedom as they earn it.* A parenting class on technology is challenging to teach. Basically, parents look panicked the entire time I'm speaking on the subject. Therefore, I try to make it as warm and fun as possible, which is not easy. I tell stories and show funny videos, and smile a lot. I was teaching one such class at a church not too long ago, when the time came for Q&A at the

end. A man in the back of the room raised his hand. I was slightly concerned, having noticed this man at different points during the class. I was highly aware that he was more than disgruntled with my philosophy on technology. When he got the microphone, he loudly said, "I have raised six children, and I just want to say—technology is NOT a child's God-given right. When we were raising my oldest son, it wasn't until we were driving him to his high school graduation that we let him get on the internet for the first time on his phone. It was also the first time we let him send someone else a picture from that phone." He stopped for a long, dramatic pause and then said, "If your child is on the internet, go home and shut it down!" And just in case someone missed his quite un-missable point, he shouted it—not once, but twice more, "IF YOUR CHILD IS ON THE INTERNET, GO HOME AND SHUT IT DOWN!!!!" All I could think to do was to say, "Why don't I close us in prayer?" and bow my head. My immediate thought was, was, "That 18 year old boy. I cannot imagine him going from no freedom at all to 3 months later, sitting in his college dorm room with every freedom in the world."

We want kids to learn responsible technology use while they're living with responsible adults. As in all things, we want to let the rope out gradually, giving them more freedom as they earn it. We start small, and let the rope out slowly…pulling it back in, not *if,* but *when* they mess up. Because they most likely will. And, as we're pulling in and letting that rope out, we want to give them clear guidelines.

CHAPTER 5

Include conversations and contracts.

§

WE CAN'T SAY ENOUGH HOW important it is to talk to your kids about all things, including technology. We are their gatekeepers, but we are also their teachers. We want them to learn to be responsible with their technology use. In doing so, we want to talk with them and help them have ownership in the process.

* *When—not if—you put monitoring software on your computer and gadgets, tell your children.* We want our kids to trust us, to believe that we're being honest. We want to have integrity and respect their privacy, and help them understand that privacy actually only applies when what they're doing is truly private. Nothing online actually is, which is one of the lessons we want them to learn. "If others can see it, so can your parents," in other words. Also, because I work with a lot of girls, I believe this full disclosure is important for another reason. If your teenager finds out that you caught him or her doing something when you were "snooping", there will be much more drama over the fact that you "violated their privacy" than what she was actually doing wrong in the first place. Again, lots of teenage girls in my office...

* *Give them a contract with each new gadget they receive.* Contracts give them ownership. As adults, when we sign our name on a

contract, we know the item we are receiving has value. We are agreeing to the terms listed under that contract. We are communicating that we understand what's expected of us, and we understand what will happen if we void the contract. We want our kids to see the same weightiness to the technology they receive. Create a contract when they receive their first tablet, or first cell phone. Outline the consequences for inappropriate use of the device on the contract. You can find examples of contracts on our blog at raisingboysandgirls.com.

+ *When your child is interacting with others online, they need to understand the same rules apply as in real life.* You can create your own list of rules to discuss with them, beginning with a few we believe are particularly important, such as:

  + Don't talk to strangers. In other words, never put personal information online about yourself, your family, or your home.

  + Virtual interactions can hurt as much as real ones. Just because you're not saying it to someone's face doesn't mean it doesn't impact them. Words hurt, whether typed or spoken. And those typed have the power to stick around, and be sent around to other friends, parents and school administrators.

  + Nothing private is ever private. Even if you send a photo to one person, they have the ability to screen shot that photo and send it to countless others. Snapchat isn't private either. Snaps can be caught and kept. Anonymity apps can be traced back to you, as well. And anything inappropriate you send or receive can cause the sender to be guilty of violating child pornography laws. For example, a teenager who takes a naked picture and sends it to another is technically guilty of committing three felony crimes.[12] Many states are in the midst of legislation to update laws around sexting. Our kids need to know the laws, and often don't.

  + Talk to you if they ever feel uncomfortable. Kids need to hear that they can always come to you, even if they've done something wrong. If someone approaches them that they don't know, even if it's on a prohibited site, you still want them to tell you. There may be consequences, but you can let them know the consequences will be worse if they don't tell you.

* A dear friend of ours, who also happens to be a school principal, has three great questions when it comes to posting on social media: Would you share this with your grandmother? Share it on the news? Want it said about you?

Teenagers' brains aren't fully developed yet. Specifically, the frontal lobe which helps them think rationally has not yet reached its adult state. Therefore, the things that seem rational and logical to us, as grown-ups, just won't be to them. We need to include conversations and contracts with every new gadget or social media platform your child uses. We want to teach them responsibility, which includes setting boundaries around their use and consequences when they violate those boundaries. In doing so, we're not only giving them ownership, but teaching them awareness, as well.

CHAPTER 6

Wherever your kids are on social media, you need to be there, too.

§

- *Pay attention to age requirements.* There are actually age restrictions when it comes to social media apps. We get questions all of the time about the magic age for various social media sites. There is, again, no magic age. But there are age guidelines given by those very apps themselves, believe it or not. Instagram, for example, is 13. Twitter, 13. Snapchat, 13—although they have a younger version called SnapKidz. Many families do not abide by the age guidelines, although the language is strong calling the age a "requirement" and stating that the guidelines are "in compliance with the Children's Online Privacy Protection Act (COPPA).
- *Take the following into consideration:*
  - Your child's maturity level. There are children we see who are mature beyond their years, and those who are very young for their age. Just because your child meets the age requirement for a certain app does not mean they're ready to use it. Pay attention to your own instincts, in terms of your child's readiness. Talk to your spouse or a trusted friend. And talk to your child. Find out why they want to use the app and tell them your concerns.
  - Their online responsibility thus far. If your child is showing readiness in terms of their maturity and they've been

responsible with their first little email account with a few close friends and family members, it may be time to take the next step. You might want to give them access to their first social media account, with much supervision by you. If they have not been responsible, they're simply proving they're not quite ready. Give them another chance and outline specifically the behavior they need to show to reach their goal. In teaching responsibility, goals and consequences are both powerful tools.

* Their emotional stability. We have two children currently in counseling at Daystar for anxiety related to the same video game. It has frightening images these kids can simply not get out of their brains. The pictures loop and loop as the kids sit in class or try to fall asleep at night. If your child is struggling with anxiety, you want to be even more vigilant in terms of what they're allowed to use regarding apps and social media. Kids who are battling anxiety tend to get images stuck in their minds. If they're depressed, the same principle applies. Kids can get ideas for self-harm and other destructive behavior from online journals and social media apps. Again, wherever your kids are, you need to be there, too—and watching.

* Their peers. The same idea applies to social media as it does to gadgets. You don't want your child to be the first, but you also don't want them to be the last to jump on every social media train. Social media is largely how teenagers communicate today. Several years ago, a mom told me, "Our family just doesn't do social media." Her daughter was 16 and significantly behind in her development. It was honestly time for her to start to connect with other kids in the way they were most frequently connecting. She had made good choices thus far and was the only one of her friends who wasn't on social media. And it was causing her to be even further behind. Keep a pulse on what your child's peers are involved in online. Hold off as long as you can, until you believe they're ready. But don't

hold off so long that they're not learning the responsibility that only you can teach under your roof.

• *Remember the default on most apps is not private.* Check the settings when your child first downloads each game or social media platform. Make sure they're set to private, and help your child learn the importance of privacy. It can also be important to ensure that they understand the consequences in place if they remove the privacy setting.

• *Anonymity apps are never helpful.* There are countless apps now where children can tell "secrets" to each other without the person who posts the secret revealing their identity. They can post photos, create groups, and share all kind of information. Basically, they can talk behind each other's backs and post hurtful content without anyone knowing where the content originated. But, again, kids are smart. One girl told me a friend of hers posted a naked photo from her room "anonymously." "What she didn't know was that lots of us have been inside her room. We recognized her bedspread, and it got out at school the next day that it was her." Nothing private online is ever truly private, and anonymity typically gets exposed.

• *Watch out for secret accounts.* Just this week, I had a group of girls talk about the prevalence of secret social media accounts. Kids create secret accounts for a variety of reasons. They want a group with just their closest friends, where they can post things others won't see. They want to be able to post things they wouldn't say under their own name. They want to post photos they wouldn't normally post, sometimes inappropriate photos. I've also heard of secret Instagram accounts just for the purpose of showing pictures of body parts they've self-harmed. Again, anonymity doesn't really work on social media. Our kids don't need to post things they wouldn't feel comfortable with everyone seeing. We're teaching responsibility online. But we're also teaching integrity. Secrecy doesn't create much of either.

- *Be aware of secrecy apps.* Secrecy apps are created to hide things: other apps, photos, etc. They often look like an empty box or even another app. Two that are popular currently look like calculators. As you start to press buttons on the calculator, whatever is hidden is revealed. It's important to be aware of the apps your child downloads, and check their phones with regularity, albeit less regularity as they get older and prove themselves responsible.
- *Loneliness doesn't show up on Instagram.* This is a sentence I tell girls almost daily in my office. Think about your own middle and high school years. Remember sitting in class and overhearing a conversation about a party to which you weren't invited? It hurt then. But how much would it hurt to see eight pictures posted by your best friends, looking like they're having the time of their lives? It happens to us, as adults. Everyone's holidays look happier, spring breaks look sunnier, lives in general can look better when it comes to social media. And our adult brains are fully developed. As we start the conversations about allowing our kids to be on social media, we also need to talk about the impact of social media. They need to understand that their feelings will be hurt. They'll feel left out. No one looks sad or lonely on social media. They also need to be aware of how easily it is to hurt others with posts. Talk to your child. Give them examples from your life. And remind them they can always come to you if they've seen something hurtful.
- *Stay current.* Make sure that you're following blogs and participating in forums to learn about the latest apps kids are using. They change with unbelievable rapidity, and we need to stay abreast of what's captivating their attention and can impact their hearts. Common Sense Media, Screenagers, and Technology Tuesday's on our blog are all resources that are committed to getting the latest information out to parents regarding technology trends with kids.

CHAPTER 7
Use it to your advantage.

§

WE DON'T WANT TO JUST see technology as a monster in the lives of the kids we love. It can also have profound impact for good. It has been cited as a tool in helping children learn critical thinking, reading comprehension, self-regulation, social skills, empathy and a variety of other important skills we want our kids to have.[13] We want to use technology to benefit the kids in our lives, and us, as adults, too.

- *Use it as a reward.* If you google "earn screen time" on Pinterest, over 1000 images come up. There are grids upon grids for children, with examples of how they can earn more time on technology when they complete their chores, or show certain behaviors we're trying to enforce. As the gentleman in my class said, technology is not a God-given right in the life of your child. But, it's one you can give them as they earn it. We want rewards that are the highest currency in the lives of kids, and technology is often where the top dollars are.
- *Use it as a consequence.* We want the highest currency in terms of both rewards *and* consequences for our kids. As soon as a child is old enough to have a device, they are old enough for that device to be used as a consequence. We're advocates at Raising Boys and Girls of immediate, short-term consequences that build on themselves. "If you continue to be disrespectful, you'll lose your iPad. ...You just lost it for an hour. ...That's another hour." If we start

off taking their gadgets for a week, we don't have any room to build, and consequences that build on themselves teach kids cause and effect. They see the direct result of their behavior.

* *Use it as a teaching tool.* Apps abound to teach kids vital tools like empathy and various social skills. They teach children to read and name emotions. They teach kids to regulate emotions, such as anger. They can also teach children to focus. Common Sense Media regularly lists their top-rated social skills building apps. We do on our blog, as well. In our newest book, *Are My Kids on Track*, we talk about the decline in kids' ability today to express, read, and regulate emotions. These are vital skills in the transition to healthy adulthood for our children. If technology can help them learn, use it to your advantage.

CHAPTER 8

They hear you some, but watch you more.

§

Or, as my friend and co-author David Thomas says in parenting seminars, "Kids learn more from observation than information." Your child is paying attention to your technology use—more attention than you have any idea.

- *Be responsible for your own technology use.* I am saddened every time I go out to eat and sit next to a parent and child, both on their devices. Put yours down, so that they'll see the importance of connection—even when they're 13 and that connection is harder to come by. Don't be tempted to pick up your phone in the car, when you're soon going to be teaching them they're not allowed to look at theirs. Bathtime and bedtime are such rich times with kids that should be uninterrupted by our technology use, as well. We have to be aware of what we're modeling.
- *Kids don't need to feel like they're competing with technology for your attention.* We're hearing more kids than ever talk about this in our offices. Their dads won't stop playing video games to hang out with them. Their moms are so busy looking at their own social media that they're not listening. Put your phone down. Look your child in the eye. And connect in real time.

- *Be aware of what you post about your child.* A dear friend of mine recently posted a naked picture of her toddler-aged daughter. I'll admit it. The picture was adorable. But I, given what I do for a living, immediately called her and told her to take it down. You can guess the reasons. Some predators don't care the age of your son or daughter. And nothing private is ever private. You also want to be aware of what you're saying about your children. Just like we tell them, anything online is actually not private and doesn't go away. 3 Questions to ask *yourself* before *you* post: Would you be okay with your child reading what you've written ten years from now? Would you have been embarrassed if your mom told all of her friends (because this is a much bigger scale)? Are you telling something that is his story to tell?

- *Be aware of what you post about yourself.* For many of the same reasons, I often read what parents write on their social media sites and worry. I worry about the child whose parents are divorcing, and reads what his mom posted about her ex-spouse. I worry about the personal information that a child does not need to know about her dad's past, now that she's a teenager and doing her own experimentation. Make sure that what you post you would not only share with your grandmother, but with your own child...because, eventually, you will.

- *Social media brings out the narcissist in us all.* How much power do likes and favorites have in your life? How much focus are you placing on your own image, due to social media? Years ago, a friend told me, "You can't ask someone to go somewhere you're not willing to go yourself." The same holds true for us and our technology and social media use. We're teaching kids not to base their self-worth on others' approval. We're teaching them to value real relationships over online relationships. We're telling them that who they are is much deeper than what they post. And that they're God's precious creation no matter what is happening around them or being reflected to them online.

We are responsible for teaching these little ones responsibility. We're given the high calling and honor of safeguarding their little hearts. We want to have integrity in this, as in all things parenting. And, mostly, we want to teach them who they really are in Christ…loved, delighted in, rejoiced over, and given more grace than they'll ever need for even their most monster-ish moments. We want to live out and love our digital natives into those kinds of truths.

Notes

§

1   Westcott, Lucy. (January 30, 2014). How Often Does The Average Person Check Their Phone? Every 10 Minutes, New Study Finds. Bustle, retrieved from https://www.bustle.com/articles/14133-how-often-does-the-average-person-check-their-phone-every-10-minutes-new-study-finds

2   Howard, Jacqueline. (July 29, 201i6). Americans devote more than 10 hours a day to screen time, and growing. CNN.com, retrieved from http://www.cnn.com/2016/06/30/health/americans-screen-time-nielsen/

3   Conrad, Dr. Brent. Media Statistics-Children's Use of TV, Internet, and Video Games. Tech Addiction, retrieved from http://www.techaddiction.ca/media-statistics.html

4   Media and Children Communication Toolkit. American Academy of Pediatrics, retrieved from https://www.aap.org/en-us/advocacy-and-policy/aap-health-initiatives/pages/media-and-children.aspx

5   Wallace, Kelly. (November 3, 2015). Teens Spend a 'mind-boggling' 9 hours a day using media, report says. CNN.com, retrieved from http://www.cnn.com/2015/11/03/health/teens-tweens-media-screen-use-report/

6   Byrne, Ciara. (January 19, 2011). Generation tech: More kids can play computer games than ride a bike. Venture Beat, retrieved from http://venturebeat.com/2011/01/19/kids-technology/

7   Rowan, Cris. (January 29, 2013). The Impact of Technology on the Developing Child. The Huffington Post, retrieved from http://www.huffingtonpost.com/cris-rowan/technology-children-negative-impact_b_3343245.html

8   Interview: Jay Giedd. Inside the Teenage Brain. Frontline. PBS.org, retrieved from http://www.pbs.org/wgbh/pages/frontline/shows/teenbrain/interviews/giedd.html

9   Wolpert, Stuart. (August 21, 2014). In our digital world, are young people losing the ability to read emotions? UCLA Newsroom, retrieved from http://newsroom.ucla.edu/releases/in-our-digital-world-are-young-people-losing-the-ability-to-read-emotions

10 Rowan, Cris. (January 29, 2013). The Impact of Technology on the Developing Child. The Huffington Post, retrieved from http://www.huffingtonpost.com/cris-rowan/technology-[11]https://www.aap.org/en-us/about-the-aap/aap-press-room/pages/american-academy-of-pediatrics-announces-new-recommendations-for-childrens-media-use.aspx

12 American Academy of Pediatrics Announces New Recommendations for Children's Media Use. (October 21, 2016). American Academy of Pediatrics, retrieved from http://www.huffingtonpost.com/dr-larry-rosen/how-much-technology-shoul_b_3142227.html

13 Rowan, Cris. (March 6, 2014). 10 Reasons Why Handheld Devices Should Be Banned for Children Under the Age of 12. The Huffington Post, retrieved from http://www.huffingtonpost.

com/cris-rowan/10-reasons-why-handheld-devices-should-be-banned_b_4899218.html

14 U.S. Sexting Laws and Regulations. Mobile Media Guard, retrieved from http://mobilemediaguard.com/state_main.html

15 Loo, Kara. (November 4, 2014). 7 Ways Video Games Will Help Your Kids in School. The Huffington post, retrieved from http://www.huffingtonpost.com/kara-loo/7-ways-video-games-help_b_6084990.html

Sɪssʏ Gᴏꜰꜰ, M.Eᴅ., LPC-MHSP sᴘᴇɴᴅs most of her days talking with girls and their families, with the help of her counseling assistant/pet therapist, Lucy the Havanese. She has worked as the Director of Child and Adolescent Counseling at Daystar Counseling Ministries in Nashville, Tennessee since 1993, with a Master's degree from Vanderbilt University. A sought-after speaker for parenting and teacher training events such as d6, MOMcon, and dotMom, Sissy has spoken to thousands of parents and teachers across the country. Sissy is the author of eight books including her newest book, *Are My Kids on Track?*, as well as *Raising Girls*. Sissy is a regular guest and contributor to media shows and publications such as *ParentLife* and *Parenting Teens* magazines.

Raising Boys and Girls is made up of Sissy, David Thomas, LMSW and Melissa Trevathan, MRE. All three are counselors with a combined 70 years of experience working with kids and families. Between the three of them, they have authored 12 books and counseled thousands of children. They continue to meet with children and families at Daystar Counseling Ministries, which one child called "the little yellow house that helps people." Daystar currently serves over 1400 families in middle-Tennessee and beyond, with a staff of thirteen counselors and three very talented pet therapists. Melissa, David, and Sissy are also sought-after speakers and have spoken to thousands of parents and teachers across the country. It is their hope that their books and seminars will be an opportunity to come alongside you in your parenting. They want to reach beyond the walls of their counseling offices at Daystar and into your homes...to encourage you, to laugh with you, to share with you what they feel is going on in the hearts of children, teens, and parents, and mostly, to bring you hope in your journey. For more information on Raising Boys and Girls' resources, or how you can bring them to speak to your community, go to raisingboysandgirls.com.